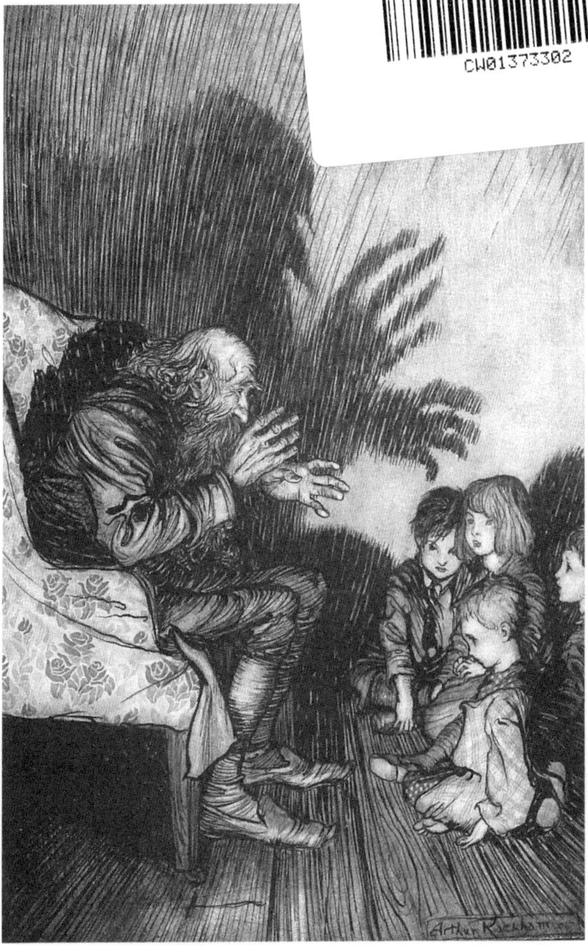
Arthur Rackham

First published 2021
© Wooden Books Ltd 2021

Published by Wooden Books Ltd.
Glastonbury, Somerset

British Library Cataloguing in Publication Data
Jones, A.
Plot

A CIP catalogue record for this book
may be obtained from the British Library

ISBN-10: 1-904263-10-0
ISBN-13: 978-1-904263-10-4

All rights reserved.
For permission to reproduce any part of this
useful little book please contact the publishers.

Designed and typeset in Glastonbury, UK.

Printed in China on 100% FSC
approved sustainable papers by FSC
RR Donnelley Asia Printing Solutions Ltd.

PLOT

THE ART OF STORY

Amy Jones

Dedicated to my brothers
And their spawn:
Darcie, Otis, Aubrey, Elliott and Louie

Recommend further reading: Aristotle, *The Poetics*; John Yorke, *Into the Woods*; Stephen King, *On Writing: A Memoir of the Craft*; Horace, *Ars Poetica*; Northrop Frye, *Anatomy of Criticism*; Syd Field, *Screenplay*; Vladimir Propp, *Morphology of the Folk Tale*; Joseph Campbell, *The Hero's Journey*; Christopher Vogler, *The Writer's Journey*; Christopher Booker, *The Seven Basic Plots*.

All cartoons remain © original copyright holders and may not be reproduced. They are licenced for this book via www.Cartoonstock.com (*pages iii, 3, 11, 39, 43, 45, 49, 55 & 58*). Other pictures are by Arthur Rackham [1867–1939] (*pages i, 18 & 29*), Gustav Doré [1832–1883] (*page vi*), Pauline Baynes [1992–2008] (*page 9*), William Wallace Denslow [1856–1915] (*page 14*), John Flaxman [1755–1826] (*pages 37 & 51*), John Tenniel [1820–1914] (*page 57*), and other 19th century illustrators.

"Shall we put it in play?"

Introduction	1
Character or Plot Driven	2
Beginning, Middle & End	4
Freytag's Pyramid	6
The Green World	8
Conflict & Opposition	10
The Well-Made Play	12
The Five-Stage Film	14
Plot Points	16
The Structure of Folk Tales	18
The Hero's Journey	20
The Shapes Stories Take	22
Seven Plots	24
Overcoming the Monster	25
Rags to Riches	26
Voyage & Return	27
The Quest	28
Tragedy	30
Comedy	32
Rebirth	33
Chronology	34
Ad Ovo & In Medias Res	36
Analepsis & Prolepsis	38
Foreshadowing	40
Anaphoric & Cataphoric	42
Twists & Reveals	44
The Cliffhanger	46
Plotted Objects	48
Lock-ins & Breakouts	50
Plotting a Plot	52
Expanding a Plot	54
Grand Openings	56
Great Endings	58

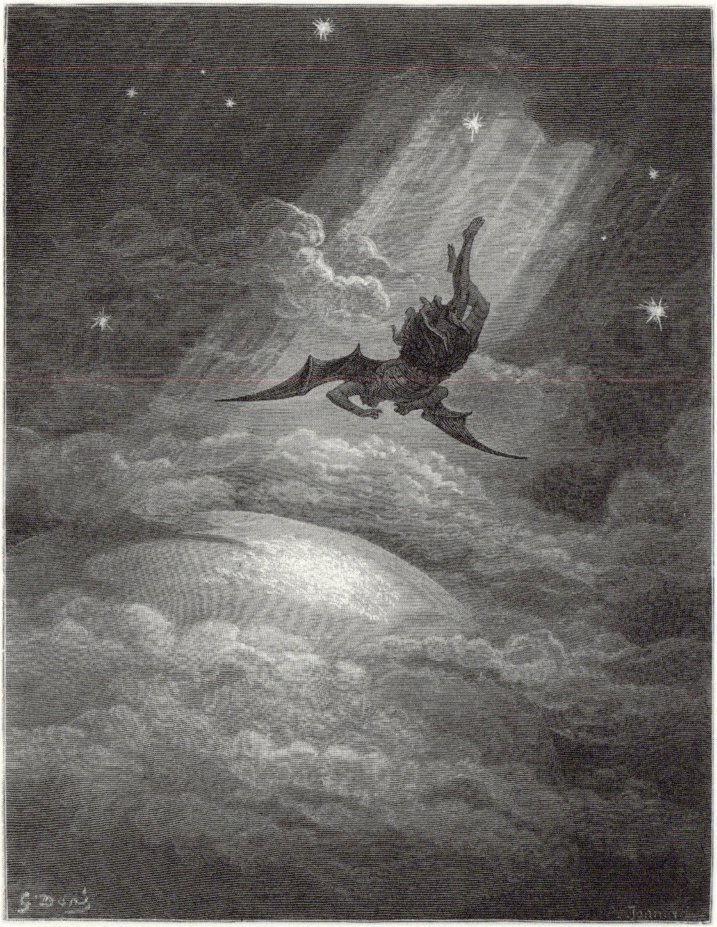

INTRODUCTION

All great stories start with the germ of an idea, an embryonic *something*. This book aims to help aspiring authors grow that original conception—be it a memory retrieved on a walk, an argument observed on a train or a fancy seen in a dream—into a well-structured work.

There are two principle components of storytelling: **STRUCTURE**, which involves the plot and framing of a story (explored in this book), and the **METHOD** of telling a story (covered in a sister book, *Narrative Voices*).

We start with theories of plot (applicable to all writers) and some specific plot models (for playwrights and screenwriters), before turning to the time-tested patterns of 'essential plots'. A section on plot and chronology and how they can be manipulated for dramatic effect is followed by advice on openings and endings, and finally some practical methods to try out.

Humans have always needed storytellers. Whether in ancient cave paintings, the oral traditions of the Aboriginal Dreamtime or the written *Epic of Gilgamesh*, African griots, Turkish ashiks and European bards have always spun their tales. Stories are more than linear accounts of events; some are visual, visceral snapshots that can transcend time and space. Other ancient tales from far-away lands can appear strange and illogical, with chains of events which do not tie together in a standard causal way. As a writer developing your own style, try to learn from all examples and appreciate the art of storytelling in all its myriad forms.

This book focuses on conventional literary structures, but you don't have to mimic these—simply learn as much as you can and grab a pen.

Are you ready? Let us begin ...

CHARACTER- OR PLOT-DRIVEN?
first steps in plotting

Once you have the germ of an idea for a story, next try to summarise the core of your plot it in a sentence or two. What are its compelling parts? What are you most interested in developing? Crucially, is your story driven mainly by character or plot? In the words of Syd Field, *All drama is conflict ... either the character drives the action, or the action drives the character.*

In a **PLOT-LED** story, the protagonist is carried along by events:

> *After a murder in a museum, two academics become involved in a battle between a secret society and the Church for an explosive secret.* The DaVinci Code, Dan Brown.

In another example, Joe Rose encounters his future stalker Jed Parry at a freak ballooning accident, presaging a disturbing chain of events:

> *We watched him drop. You could see the acceleration. No forgiveness, no special dispensation for flesh, or bravery, or kindness. Only ruthless gravity. And from somewhere, perhaps from him, perhaps from some indifferent crow, a thin squawk cut through the stilled air. He fell as he had hung, a stiff little black stick. I've never seen such a terrible thing as that falling man.* Ian McEwan, Enduring Love

Plot-led stories often move apace, naturally engaging the reader. Many open *in media res* (*see page 42*), swiftly bringing the reader to the action.

A **CHARACTER-LED** plot focuses on character development in what might or might not be an entirely normal environment. Charlotte Bronte's eponymous *Jane Eyre* is a classic example of a **BILDUNGSROMAN** (from the German *Bildung* for 'education' and *Roman* meaning 'novel') a literary genre in which the psychological and moral growth of the protagonist (the central character) is tracked from childhood into adulthood.

J.D. Salinger's *Catcher in the Rye* and Albert Camus' *L'Étranger* (*The Stranger*) are other superb examples of the way plot can operate in the service of character. In these books it is the protagonist's observations and responses—in short *who they are*—that drives the narrative:

> I summarized The Stranger a long time ago, with a remark I admit was highly paradoxical: "In our society any man who does not weep at his mother's funeral runs the risk of being sentenced to death." I only meant that the hero of my book is condemned because he does not play the game. Albert Camus.

Your next step is to produce a short **OVERVIEW**. Sketch out your central characters and their relationships to one another, and stake out the key plot points in your story like fence posts in the ground. Later, when you write the narrative, you will be stringing wires from one post to the next, but at this stage don't get distracted by narrative devices, non-linear chronologies or interesting language. The overview should be a two-page document that you can refer back to later, when you get lost in the labyrinth of your own words.

"I forget, is this the show with the back stabbing, or the front stabbing?"

BEGINNING, MIDDLE & END
Aristotle and the three-act structure

To help navigate the world of plot, let's go back to the beginning. In his *Poetics*, the Greek philosopher Aristotle [384–322 BC] describes the art of writing **DRAMATIC** poetry for **TRAGEDY**, **COMEDY** and **SATYR** plays, and in **LYRIC** and **EPIC** forms. Causality is central to plot, he argues. One event must clearly lead to another. Aristotle also observed that *A story that is whole has a beginning, middle and an end*, neatly establishing the **THREE ACT STRUCTURE** that underpins many Western plots to this day.

The *Poetics* likens a good story to a knot, with the two most important events in the plot being the **COMPLICATION**, in which a knot is tied, and the **UNRAVELLING** (or **DENOUEMENT**) in which it is untangled:

> *By the Complication I mean all that extends from the beginning of the action to the part which marks the turning-point to good or bad fortune. The Unravelling is that which extends from the beginning of the change to the end ... Many poets tie the knot well, but unravel it ill.*

Aristotle also highlights certain special moments in a story, the most powerful being **PERIPETEIA**—*A change by which the action veers round to its opposite*. Such reversals of fortune can result in terror, mercy, laughter or tears. A poor character may become rich or vice, versa.

In a tragedy, the protagonist often makes a misstep due to a character flaw (their **HAMARTIA**), which then has consequences. In *Hamlet*, the peripeteia occurs when he mistakenly kills Polonius, precipitating his downfall. In *Oedipus Rex*, Aristotle identifies the peripeteia as

> *... when the messenger comes to cheer Oedipus and free him from his alarms about his mother, but by revealing who he is, he produces the opposite effect.*

Another key element of tragedy, says Aristotle, is **ANAGNORISIS**, a moment of realisation, when the Protagonist recognises what is happening but is powerless to stop it, despite a change of heart. This heightens the pity and fear in an audience, helping build towards the final **CATHARSIS**, a purifying outpouring of emotions.

Aristotle's division of a tale into beginning, middle and end, with key moments driving the story, remains the basis of narrative theory to this day. Here is a modern take on it, with elements we will meet again soon:

ACT 1: SETUP
EXPOSITION. *The key characters are established in their everyday world.*
COMPLICATION. *An event rocks the boat and sets the story in motion.*
PLOT POINT 1. *The protagonist decides to tackle the challenge.*

ACT 2: CONFRONTATION
RISING ACTION. *The stakes grow higher. Encounters with enemies and allies.*
MIDPOINT. *Something disrupts the protagonist's mission.*
PLOT POINT 2. *The protagonist is tested. Success is in doubt.*

ACT 3: RESOLUTION
PRE CLIMAX. *Always darkest before dawn, the protagonist must act or fail.*
CLIMAX. *The final showdown, for better or worse.*
END. *All loose ends are tied up. A new equilibrium is established.*

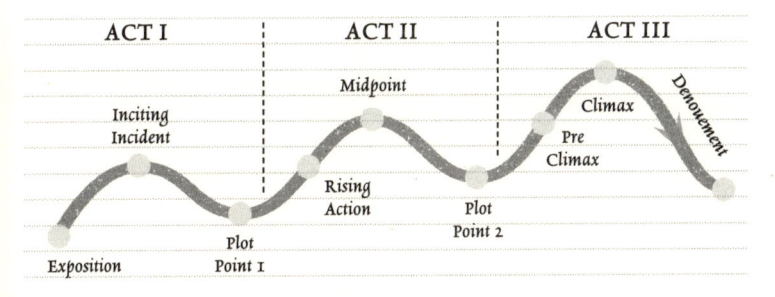

Freytag's Pyramid
rising and falling

The Roman writer Horace [65–8 BC] was an early dramatic theorist. In his *Ars Poetica*, building on Aristotle's ideas, he advocates a **Five Act Structure**. The German novelist Gustav Freytag [1816–1895] also divided stories into five parts (*drawn as a pyramid, below*), and included an **Inciting Incident** (Aristotle's knot-tying) and a **Resolution** (the unravelling).

1. **The Exposition** introduces key characters, themes, and settings.

2. **The Rising Action** builds on an *inciting incident*—a significant event (e.g. future lovers meeting, a murder, a revealing letter). A mystery or challenge creates anticipation, and the protagonists respond.

3. **The Climax** resolves rising tensions, providing a level of satisfaction, usually through a dramatic scene. It pulls together strands laid down earlier in the narrative, usually in a short space of time.

4. **Falling Action** sees characters react to the climax and work towards a *resolution*, with all events and loose ends addressed.

5. **The Denouement** completes the story arc, creating closure, enabling the characters and audience to move on (e.g. marriage, drive off, death).

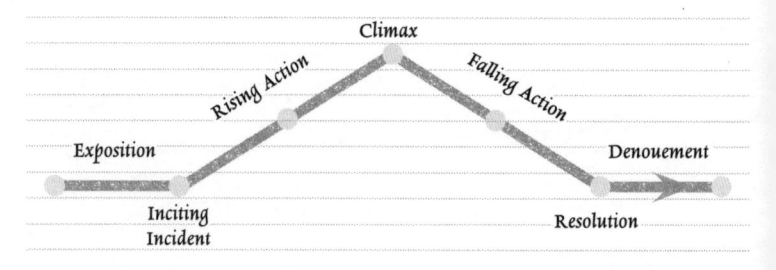

Applied to Agatha Christie's *Murder on the Orient Express*, Freytag's pyramid may look like this [spoiler alert]:

1. POIROT *travels to London on the Orient Express.* – EXPOSITION
I. *He is awakened by a scream in the night.* – INCITING INCIDENT
2. *Poirot hears another strange noise. A passenger claims that someone has been in her compartment. The train gets stuck in a snowbank.* – RISING ACTION
3. *One passenger, Ratchett, is found horribly murdered.* – CLIMAX
4. *Poirot investigates, and reveals that Ratchett was really Cassetti, an evil gang leader who had kidnapped and murdered a 3-year-old girl. The 12 passengers had arranged to meet on the train and kill him in revenge.* – FALLING ACTION
R. *Poirot presents two solutions to officials M. Bouc and Dr. Constantine, one a false but plausible account, the other the truth.* – RESOLUTION
5. *The false account is accepted and will be relayed to the police. The killers are allowed to go free.* – DENOUEMENT

Or, perhaps the discovery of the body is the true inciting incident and the climax is really the scene in which the perpetrators are unmasked. Perhaps there are actually several triangles ...

Indeed, for most serialised works, such as television and radio shows, a single broad narrative arc follows Freytag's pyramid across the entire series, but then smaller pyramid structures within each season and each episode keep the audience engaged and satisfied, and wanting to come back for more.

THE GREEN WORLD
leaving the old, returning renewed

When narratives enter unrealistic or supernatural situations, they maintain a remarkable degree of mimetic realism. The literary theorist Northrop Frye [1912–1991] explains this by claiming we inhabit two worlds. In the words of author Ian McEwan:

> *We spend our lives partly in a waking world we call normal and partly in a dream world which we create of our own desires.* Ian McEwan, The Argument of Comedy

Shakespeare uses this in his dramatic works, argues Frye. He endows

> *both worlds with equal imaginative power, brings them opposite one another, and makes each world seem unreal when seen by the light of the other ...*

Thus, comedies such as *Twelfth Night* and *A Midsummer Night's Dream* begin in a recognisable world, then shift to one that is removed—called by Frye the 'green world'—before returning back to 'normal' reality. So, for Frye, this journey involves three worlds:

THE OLD WORLD is dominated by older, parental figures, often repressive, restrictive and urban. We may glimpse it at the beginning or it may simply be referred to. In Act 1 Scene 1 of *A Midsummer Night's Dream*, we are presented with Egeus attempting to control who his daughter, Hermia, marries: *Full of vexation come I, with complaint / Against my child, my daughter Hermia*. We are then swiftly transported into:

THE GREEN WORLD, often literally green, e.g. a forest. A place of freedom (for characters and writers), liberated from strict moral values and mimesis of reality; a world infused with magic, mystery, delight and confusion. Hermia and other young characters enter the forest realm of Titania,

Oberon and Puck. Chaos ensues, with magical transfigurations, love potions, mix-ups, fights and hilarity as the play enters Act 2 and the fairy King Oberon commands his servant Puck to begin his work: *There sleeps Titania sometime of the night / Lull'd in these flowers with dances and delight.* With so much chaos and disorder, time in the green world can only be fleeting.

THE NEW WORLD occurs in what Freytag would call the denouement (*see pages 6-7*). Our characters return to the sensible, ordered world, significantly changed. Darker forces have been dispelled. Out of their parents' shadow they make their own decisions: *So shall all the couples three / Ever true in loving be; / And the blots of Nature's hand / Shall not in their issue stand.* Keen to re-establish a sense of order for his audience, Shakespeare gives Puck the final lines, *If we shadows have offended, / Think but this, and all is mended, / That you have but slumber'd here / While these visions did appear.*

Frye's theory can be widely applied. In the 1986 Jim Henson film *Labyrinth*, the old world of the young protagonist Jennifer consists of conflict and resentment. The labyrinth, magical and dangerous, offers her escape and redemption. At the core of the narrative is a girl transitioning into womanhood, the green world structure a metaphor for growing up.

In C. S. Lewis' *The Lion, The Witch and the Wardrobe*, four young people are evacuated during the war (an artifact of the older generation) from the city to the countryside, and then to Narnia, before returning to the new world, wiser and more mature.

Maurice Sendak's *Where the Wild Things Are* is another classic example.

CONFLICT & OPPOSITION
into the woods

The traits of good stories seem to be universal. Indeed, the three-act drama, described by Aristotle over 2000 years ago (*see page 4*), remains the basic form today. Why is this? Perhaps, argues literary theorist John Yorke, it is because we all learn this structure in childhood:

> **THESIS:** *A child explores the world with no knowledge of it.*
> **ANTITHESIS:** *She encounters a flame, a potentially destructive opposite.*
> **SYNTHESIS:** *Burnt by the flame, she synthesises the knowledge that fire is bad, and learns from the experience.*

Compare this with a simple standard story of the same form:

> **THESIS:** *A character goes on a journey.*
> **ANTITHESIS:** *They encounter their opposite.*
> **SYNTHESIS:** *Each assimilates the other's qualities and the process starts again.*

Opposites are crucial, says Yorke. Just as one cannot understand the meaning of good without knowing evil, **All character, all structure, all drama, is built on the law of opposites.** Thus, conflict and opposition are found *between* characters (e.g. criminal *vs* detective, or hunter *vs* prey) and also *within* them (e.g. the literary trope of **APPEARANCE *vs* REALITY**, where the 'purer' an individual presents themselves, the darker they are in reality).

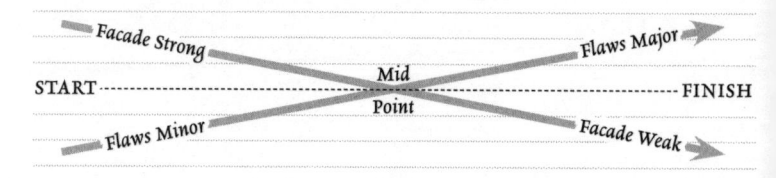

The stronger the stance, the stronger the opposition, and as the narrative progresses, opposites are drawn together, ideologically and dramatically, to converge in conflict (*the midpoint in the diagram opposite*), producing order from chaos and restoring Todorov's equilibrium (*see page* 14).

In Nathaniel Hawthorn's *The Scarlet Letter*, Rev. Dimmesdale spends years hiding the fact he fathered a child with a woman called Hester, while she is forced to wear an humiliating scarlet 'A' for adultery. Dimmesdale wrestles with his conscience, until SECRET and TRUTH synthesise:

> "People of New England!" cried he with a voice that rose over them, high, solemn, and majestic, — yet had always a tremor through it … "ye, that have loved me! — ye, that have deemed me holy! — behold me here, the one sinner of the world!"

Other examples of respected facades that quickly crumble include the dutiful son and war hero Michael Corleone at the beginning of *The Godfather*, and Walter White in the 2008 *Breaking Bad* series.

Yorke recommends writers ask ten questions of a story:

1. Whose story is this?
2. What do they need?
3. What is the inciting incident?
4. What does the protagonist want?
5. What obstacles are in the way?
6. What's at stake?
7. Why should we care?
8. What does the protagonist learn?
9. How and why do they learn this?
10. How does the story end?

"He's his own worst enemy."

THE WELL-MADE PLAY
oven-ready plots

In the 19th century, French dramatists Eugène Scribe [1791–1861] and Victorien Sardou [1831–1908] built on Aristotle's tragic structure to create a popular plotting template, the **WELL-MADE PLAY**. In these dramas, characters often hide interconnected secrets, with importance placed on physical objects (e.g. letters, jewellery, gloves or handbags) to move events along. There is high **DRAMATIC IRONY**. Characters enter and exit the stage in tense near-misses, acts end with climatic **STRONG CURTAINS** and the action builds to a sensational final revelation. As English dramatist Wilkie Collins [1824-1889] said: *Make 'em laugh; make 'em weep; make 'em wait.*

By the late 1900s, the well-made play had became a byword for formulaic scriptwriting. As a result, dramatists like J.B. Priestley (*An Inspector Calls*) and Oscar Wilde (*The Importance of Being Earnest*) made significant structural adaptations, and **REALIST** playwrights, such as Henrik Ibsen [1828-1906], deliberately defied many of its conventions, while keeping the basic structure and many of the plot devices (*see example opposite*).

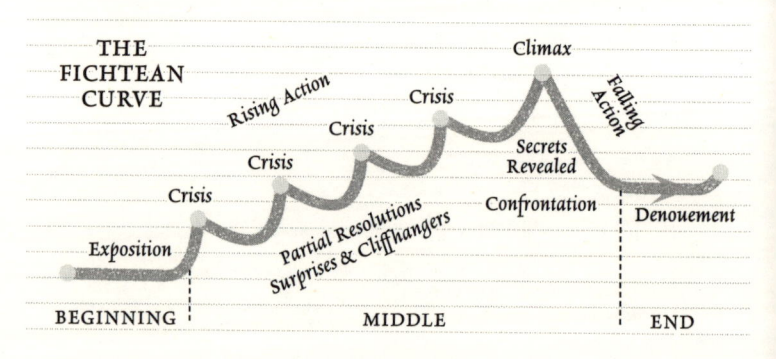

THE FICHTEAN CURVE

Beginning: Exposition, Crisis
Middle: Rising Action, Crisis, Crisis, Crisis, Partial Resolutions, Surprises & Cliffhangers, Climax, Falling Action, Secrets Revealed, Confrontation
End: Denouement

A DOLL'S HOUSE by HENRIK IBSEN

A well-made play, first performed in 1879.
Actions and objects common to this genre have been CAPITALISED.

ACT 1. EXPOSITION

Nora Helmer once SECRETLY borrowed a large sum of money so her husband Torvald could recuperate from illness. She has been SECRETLY paying it back in installments ever since. Torvald WRONGLY THINKS her careless and childlike, and often calls her his doll. When he is appointed director at the bank, his first act is to relieve a man who was once DISGRACED for having FORGED A SIGNATURE on a DOCUMENT. This man, Nils Krogstad, is the person from whom Nora borrowed her money. It is also REVEALED that in order to get the money SHE FORGED A SIGNATURE. Krogstad THREATENS TO REVEAL Nora's CRIME and DISGRACE her and her husband unless Nora can convince Torvald not to fire him. Much SUSPENSE. STRONG CURTAIN.

ACT 2. DEVELOPMENT AND COMPLICATION

Nora STRUGGLES TO FIND A WAY OUT but Torvald sends Krogstad the A LETTER of dismissal. Nora considers asking her husband's friend Dr Rank for HELP but he merely CONFESSES LOVE for her. CRISIS as ALL POSSIBLE SOLUTIONS FAIL. Her tarantella dance, a FRANTIC ATTEMPT to POSTPONE THE READING of Krogstad's TELL-ALL reply LETTER, makes a DRAMATIC CURTAIN.

ACT 3. TOWARDS THE CLIMAX AND DENOUEMENT.

MORE SUSPENSE with HINTS that a RESOLUTION COULD HAPPEN AFTER ALL. Krogstad's former lover Kristine offers him REDEMPTION and he has a CHANGE OF HEART, the LETTER COULD BE DESTROYED. Dr Rank DELAYS THE READING OF THE LETTER. Then the CLIMAX, the CONFRONTATION between Nora and Torvald (the scène à faire EAGERLY EXPECTED since the first act). Torvald reads the letter, Nora's SECRET is finally REVEALED. Torvald is enraged and thinks only of himself. DENOUEMENT: All is solved! Krogstad posts the INCRIMINATING DOCUMENT to Torvald, who now speaks of forgiveness. But Nora sees that he is unworthy of her love and announces that she will leave him (and the children).

A shocking, hardly happy, ending. An audience of the day used to the conventions of the genre would have expected a husband to have been forgiving *before* the situation was saved.
The play was groundbreaking for its time and remains a classic to this day.

THE FIVE-STAGE FILM
Todorov's lesson in structure

Plays may follow time-tested formulae, but do films work the same way? In the 1960s, Bulgarian literary critic and cultural theorist Tzvetan Todorov [1939-2017] analysed the plot structures of popular films and identified five stages through which many of their narratives progressed:

1. **EQUILIBRIUM** - *Everything is as it should be and the characters lives are normal.*
2. **DISRUPTION** - *An event disturbs the equilibrium into disequilibrium.*
3. **RECOGNITION** - *There is a realisation that disorder has occurred.*
4. **ACTION** - *to resolve or fix the damage or disruption.*
5. **RESTORATION** - *A new equilibrium is found.*

Torodov's structure is not dissimilar to Freytag's Pyramid (*page 6*), or Frye's Three Worlds (*page 8*). It can be used as a writing tool, or for analysis. Here it is applied to the 1939 film *The Wonderful Wizard of Oz*:

1. **EQUILIBRIUM** - *Dorothy leads a normal life on a farm in Kansas.*
2. **DISRUPTION** - *A tornado picks up the family home and flies Dorothy and Toto to a magical otherworld - Oz.*

3. RECOGNITION - Dorothy and Toto are not in Kansas anymore! The house landing killed the Wicked Witch of the East, and they are now the enemies of her vengeful sister, the Wicked Witch of the West. They must get home, at all cost!

4. ACTION - Dorothy is advised to go to Emerald City and ask the Wizard of Oz for help. Along the way they she and Toto meet three new friends and face different obstacles together. At the climax the Witch of the West is defeated, the wizard is exposed as an ordinary man and Dorothy clicks her heels to get home.

5. RESTORATION - Dorothy wakes up back in Kansas surrounded by her family. It seems like nothing has changed ….

Slight variations on Torodov's structure are also useful. Here is a popular one, which compresses the disruption and recognition, and expands the action, as applied to Edgar Wright's 2004 film, *Shaun of the Dead*:

1. EQUILIBRIUM - Shaun, an unambitious loser, and Ed, his lazy best mate, love the pub. Shaun is hopeless with his girlfriend, Liz, and hates his stepfather.

2. DISRUPTION & REALISATION - We begin to notice an outbreak of flesh-eating zombies. In a garden, Shaun and Ed finally clock the situation and realise what they need to do.

3. ACTION - They rescue Liz and Shaun's parents, and decide to hole up in the pub until the situation improves. They survive increasingly intense attacks by zombies.

4. RESOLUTION - The army arrive and kill all the zombies.

5. RESTORATION - Shaun and Liz are happy. Ed has become a zombie but he and Shaun are still mates. Zombies are used for entertainment.

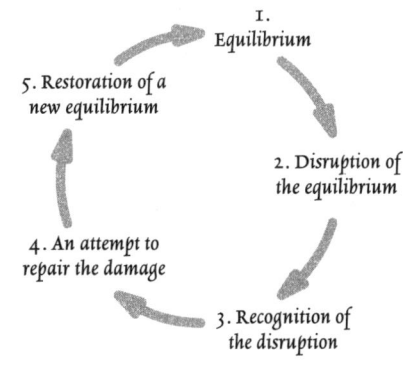

1. Equilibrium
2. Disruption of the equilibrium
3. Recognition of the disruption
4. An attempt to repair the damage
5. Restoration of a new equilibrium

PLOT POINTS
riveting the story together

Any event in a story can be important, but certain key events really move the story forward and are especially significant. These are known as **PLOT POINTS**, and we have already met one of them, the INCITING INCIDENT (*on page 6*). Dramatic theorist Syd Field [1935–2013] describes another:

> *Dramatic structure is the foundation of screenwriting ... Simply put, structure holds the story together; there is a beginning, middle and end, (not necessarily in that order), and a point at which the beginning turns into the middle, or the middle turns into the end. That point is called a* PLOT POINT. *It is any incident, episode or event that hooks into the action and spins it around into another direction; in this case, either Act II or Act III. There are many plot points in a screenplay, but in the creation of the story line, the most important are Plot Point I and Plot Point II. The four elements of structure, Beginning, Plot Point I, Plot Point II and the Ending, will always hold your story in place.* Screenplay, Syd Field.

THE SHAWSHANK REDEMPTION

ACT I	ACT II FIRST HALF	ACT II SECOND HALF	ACT III
Andy convicted. Enters Shawshank	Andy makes friends with Red and adapts to prison life	Andy passes his knowledge on to other inmates	Andy and Red reunite in Mexico
PLOT POINT 1 Andy asks Red for a rock hammer	MIDPOINT Andy plays opera arias over prison PA		PLOT POINT 2 Andy escapes from prison
SET-UP 25 mins	CONFRONTATION 50 mins		RESOLUTION 15 mins

Field designed a diagram for plotting film narratives, known as *Syd Field's Paradigm*. As an example, he fills in his sheet for the 1994 film of the Stephen King novella *The Shawshank Redemption* (*facing page*).

In a bad story, events are unconnected: *This happens, then this happens, oh then this happens*. In a good story, events are riveted together and driven by plot points: *This happens, so this happens, but then this happens too, so this has to happen*. Some plots only require two plot points, while others use more. Author Dan Wells' SEVEN-POINT STORY STRUCTURE builds on Field's Paradigm (*illustrated below*), while screenwriter Dave Trottier's MAGNIFICENT SEVEN plot points have a slightly different rhythm. Below, we combine both:

A. THE BACK STORY: *Current situation. Something haunts the main character.*
B. THE CATALYST: *A call to adventure starts the narrative and character development.*
C. THE BIG EVENT: *Something goes wrong, or otherwise changes the character's life.*
D. THE MIDPOINT: *They cross a point of no return, becoming active instead of passive.*
E. THE CRISIS: *Something goes badly wrong, another low point that forces a decision.*
F. THE CLIMAX: *The final showdown. They find the key to solving the conflict.*
G. RESOLUTION. *The conflict is resolved. The main character realises they are transformed.*

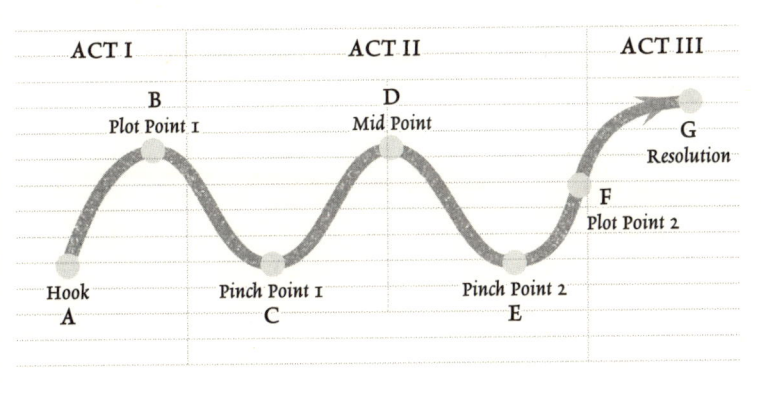

The Structure of Folk Tales
Vladimir Propp

Some of the oldest stories in the world are folk tales, and many of their themes are truly timeless. Folklorist Vladimir Propp [1895–1970] studied hundreds of Russian folk tales, or *czazka*, from which he derived 31 **NARRATIVE FUNCTIONS** or common plot devices (*shown opposite*), many of which are still used today:

> *A tale usually begins with an initial situation. The members of a family are enumerated, or the future hero (e.g., a soldier) is introduced by mention of his name or indication of his status.* Morphology of the Folk Tale, 1928

Propp focused on the sequential structure of folktales. Later theorists such as Claude Levi Strauss [1908–2009] examined features drawn *across* narratives. Building on the work of Swiss linguist Ferdinand de Saussure [1857–1913], Levi Strauss proposed that the majority of narratives are built on opposites (*see page 10*). A superhero film, for example, can be boiled down to good *vs* evil, Gothic stories are human *vs* supernatural, etc.

Swiss psychologist Carl Jung [1875–1961] and his colleague Marie-Louise von Franz [1915–1998] spent many years studying fairy tales. These ancient stories are, said Jung,

> *... the purest and simplest expression of collective unconscious processes ... they represent the archetypes in their simplest, barest and most concise form ... The fairy tale itself is its own best explanation; that is, its meaning is contained in the totality of its motifs connected by the thread of the story.*

Plot Devices in Folk Tales

0. THE INITIAL SITUATION: Exposition or setup.

1. ABANDONMENT: A member of the hero's community / family leaves home or dies.

2. EDICT: A command is set up: You dare not go there! / Do this! / Beware of that!

3. THE EDICT IS VIOLATED: Someone breaks the big rule. A villain enters the story at this point.

4. RECONNAISSANCE: The villain spies on the hero or the hero learns about the villain.

5. INFORMATION RECEIVED: The villain gains information about his victim/s.

6. TRICKERY: The villain attempts to deceive or take possession of the hero / their belongings.

7. COMPLICITY: The hero is forced or tricked to do something bad, which has bad consequences.

8. VILLAINY or LACKING: The villain causes harm or injury to a family member. AND/OR a protagonist finds they are lacking something.

9. HERO ALERTED: The Hero finds out about the villainous bad stuff and starts to form a plan.

10. COUNTERACTION: The hero chooses to thwart the villain, perhaps by seeking a magical item, rescuing those who are captured etc.

11. DEPARTURE: The hero leaves the safety of home. By choice or by force. Their adventure begins.

12. THE HELPER: The hero encounters a magical agent or helper (donor), and is tested in some manner, e.g. combat, puzzles or and so on.

13. THE HERO REACTS: Withstands a test / fails in some manner / frees a captive / reconciles disputing parties or performs good services.

14. RECEIPT OF A MAGICAL AGENT: The hero acquires use of magic as a consequence of their good actions / meeting with the donor.

15. GUIDANCE: The hero is transferred or led to a vital new location, e.g. home of the donor / villain.

16. STRUGGLE: The hero and the villain fight.

17. BRANDING: The hero is marked, perhaps scarred, or granted a cosmetic item like a ring or scarf.

18. VICTORY: The hero kills, outperforms, strikes when vulnerable, or banishes, the villain.

19. RESOLUTION: The earlier misfortunes or issues of the story are resolved; objects of search are distributed, spells broken, captives freed etc.

20. RETURN: The hero travels back home.

21. THE HERO IS PURSUED: An adversary seeks to capture, harm or eat them!

22. THE HERO IS RESCUED

23. UNRECOGNISED ARRIVAL: The hero arrives, either at their destination or somewhere en route, and is unrecognised or unacknowledged.

24. UNFOUNDED CLAIMS: A false hero presents they saved the day, or some other kind of deceit.

25. DIFFICULT TASK: The hero undergoes a trial: riddles, test of strength, acrobatics, and so on.

26. THE TASK IS RESOLVED

27. THE HERO IS RECOGNIZED: Usually by means of their prior branding.

28. FALSE HERO / VILLAIN EXPOSED

29. TRANSFIGURATION: The hero gains a new appearance / magically improves their looks!

30. THE VILLAIN IS PUNISHED

31. THE WEDDING: The hero marries the prince(ss).

THE HERO'S JOURNEY
and the heroine's journey

The world's great myths are some of the finest examples of storytelling to survive from antiquity. In the 1940s, comparative mythologist Joseph Campbell [1904–1987] realised that many heroes of these epics undergo remarkably similar journeys, both inwardly and outwardly, echoing Aristotle's core structure. A follower of the work of Carl Jung, he began to notice how the 'ego consciousness' of these heroes were often tested by an opposite 'shadow' figure, and a female 'anima' or a male 'animus'.

> *The meeting with the goddess (who is incarnate in every woman) is the final test of the talent of the hero to win the boon of love (charity: amor fati), which is life itself enjoyed as the encasement of eternity.* The Hero's Journey, 1949

Campbell concluded, like Jung, that *All the stories in the world are really one story*, a *monomyth*. He described the story of the hero over three stages, DEPARTURE, INITIATION and RETURN, with specific events in each, 17 in all (*below*). The table (*opposite*) shows a popular 1992 reworking by Christopher Vogler. This outline has been used as the backbone of countless books, movies and television series, from *Moby Dick*, to *Star Wars* to *The Matrix*.

In 1990, one of Campbell's students, Maureen Murdock, published a parallel version of the template for women, *The Heroine's Journey*, which was further developed by author Victoria Lynn Schmidt (*see opposite*).

THE HERO'S JOURNEY
1. The call to adventure
2. Refusal of the call
3. Supernatural Aid
4. Crossing the threshold
5. Belly of the whale
6. The road of trial
7. Meeting with the goddess
8. Woman as temptress
9. Atonement with the father
10. The point of realisation
11. The ultimate boon
12. Refusal of the return
13. Magic flight
14. Rescue from without
15. The return
16. Master of two worlds
17. Freedom to live

| THE HERO'S JOURNEY | THE HEROINE'S JOURNEY |
| Vogler's version, applied to *The Hobbit* | SCHMIDT/Murdock fusion, e.g. *Moana* |

1. ORDINARY WORLD:
Bilbo, an ordinary hobbit, lives in The Shire.

2. CALL TO ADVENTURE:
Gandalf seeks someone for an adventure.

3. REFUSAL OF THE CALL:
Bilbo declines but invites Gandalf for tea.

4. MEETING THE MENTOR:
Gandalf inspires Bilbo, Bilbo dreams of adventure.

5. THE FIRST THRESHOLD:
Bilbo packs his bags and leaves the Shire.

1. ILLUSION OF THE PERFECT WORLD:
The heroine naively identifies with outer masculine values, embracing the masculine ideal of perfection.

2. BETRAYAL / DISILLUSIONMENT:
In her quest for success and status, the heroine faces inner and outer obstacles, triumphing over all, while betraying her own feminine values to achieve her goal.

3. THE AWAKENING:
Her perfect world is shattered by some event. The masculine world is broken. The heroine knows she cannot remain in the illusion. She looks for assistance.

DEPARTURE

---

6. TESTS, ALLIES, ENEMIES:
Bilbo encounters trolls, elves, goblins, Gollum. Befriends Beorn and the elves.

7. THE INMOST CAVE:
Bilbo and co. approach the Lonely Mountain.

8. THE ORDEAL:
Bilbo approaches Smaug, the dragon in the cavern and steals the Arkenstone.

9. REWARD:
Smaug is killed. The dwarves occupy Lonely Mountain and its treasure. Bilbo is rich.

4. THE DESCENT / JUDGEMENT:
Meeting with the Goddess. Another crisis. Her masculine traits fail. The heroine is inspired to return to the feminine, but feels ashamed of her new identity.

5. EYE OF THE STORM:
The heroine experiences short-lived successes but is regularly undermined by people around her. She attempts to return to her earlier life, but can't.

6. ALL IS LOST / DEATH:
The situation deteriorates. The heroine's new skills fail her and she has no choice but to accept defeat.

INITIATION

---

10. THE ROAD BACK:
Instead of going home, Bilbo decides to help the dwarves regain their honour.

11. THE RESURRECTION
Battle of the five armies. Bilbo fights well, but loses consciousness.

12. RETURN WITH ELIXIR
Bilbo returns home with his share of the treasure, some newly gained wisdom, and a magic ring.

7. SUPPORT:
The heroine receives assistance from a supporter, a friend, goddess or spirit, learning that she can't do it alone. She begins to heal her wounded masculine.

8. REBIRTH / MOMENT OF TRUTH:
The heroine finds new courage and hope, integrating her masculine and feminine to speak truth with authority.

9. RETURN TO A NEW WORLD:
The heroine becomes a spiritual warrior. She now sees the world as it truly is and finds her new place in it.

RETURN

THE SHAPES STORIES TAKE
Vonnegut's essential plots

The idea that there are only a small number of plots was explored by the novelist Kurt Vonnegut [1922–2007]. Using graphs of fortune over time, Vonnegut was able to see the shape of any story at a glance.

According to Vonnegut, most stories begin with a protagonist in a comfortable or neutral position, ready to lose it all or face some life-changing event. Two simple examples illustrate his method (*graphs shown below*):

MAN IN HOLE - *The story needn't be about a man or a hole. It's: Somebody gets into trouble; gets out of it again. It is not accidental that the line ends up higher than where it began. This is encouraging to readers.*

BOY MEETS GIRL. *This needn't be about a boy meeting a girl. It's somebody, an ordinary person, on a day like any other day, comes across something perfectly wonderful: "Oh boy, this is my lucky day!" Then "Shit!" And gets back up again.*

To demonstrate an up-down-up reversal of fortunes pattern, Vonnegut chooses the classic fairy story of Cinderella (*graph on facing page*):

CINDERELLA - *A girl's mother had died, and her father remarried a battle-axe. Things can't get any worse. Her fairy godmother shows up, gives her shoes, stocking, mascara, and transport to a ball, where she dances with the prince. But*

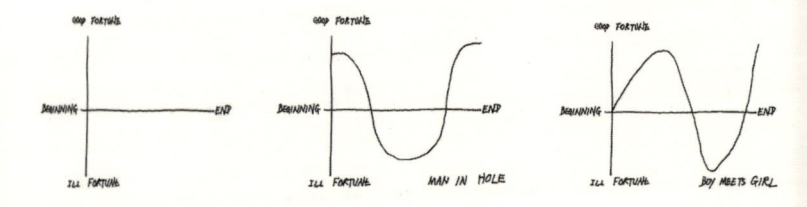

> at midnight she loses it all. Does she drop down to the same level? Hell, no! No matter what happens after that, she'll remember the prince loved her when she was the belle of the ball. Then the shoe fits and she becomes off-scale happy.

Vonnegut compares the Cinderella structure with biblical stories. For example, the life of Jesus involves gradual steps up to his position as an influential holy man, followed by crucifixion and eventual resurrection.

For a structure that starts low and gets even worse, Vonnegut turns to Franz Kafka's masterpiece *Metamorphosis* (*illustrated below*):

> METAMORPHOSIS - *A young man is rather unattractive and not very personable. He has disagreeable relatives and has had a lot of jobs with no chance of promotion. He doesn't get paid enough to take his girl dancing or to go to the beer hall to have a beer with a friend. One morning he wakes up, it's time to go to work again, and he has turned into a cockroach. It's a pessimistic story.*

For a flat story, he chooses *Hamlet*, arguing that we don't really know what's good and bad news in Shakespeare's famous story. For example, is it good or bad news that Hamlet sees a ghost who tells him:

> HAMLET! *I'm your father, I was murdered, you gotta avenge me, it was your uncle did it, here's how... There's a reason we recognize Hamlet as a masterpiece: it's that Shakespeare told us the truth, and people so rarely tell us the truth in this rise and fall here. The truth is, we know so little about life, we don't really know what the good news is and what the bad news is ... Did he go to heaven or did he go to hell?* Kurt Vonnegut, On the Shapes of Stories.

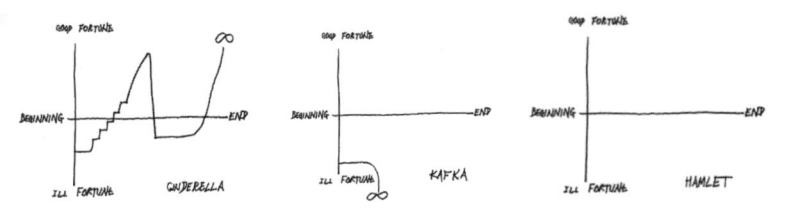

SEVEN PLOTS
to rule them all

Perhaps the most exhaustive study of plot was made by the journalist Christopher Booker [1937–2019]. After analysing hundreds of stories, he concluded that there are just seven basic plots: 1. Overcoming the Monster; 2. Rags to Riches; 3. Voyage and Return; 4. The Quest; 5. Tragedy; 6. Rebirth; 7. Comedy. All have a metanarrative of one central hero:

> *Each begins with a hero, or heroes, in some way unfulfilled. The mood at the beginning of the story is one of anticipation, as the hero seems to be standing on the edge of some great adventure or experience. In each case he finds a focus for his ambitions or desires, and for a time seems to enjoy almost dream-like success.*
>
> Christopher Booker, *The Seven Basic Plots*, 2004

Over the next few pages, we will explore each of these plots in turn. If you are writing a story, find out what your central character wants, what they need to feel fulfilled, and decide how, where and when you might give it to them (*see Yorke's questions on page 11*). This desire will be the motivation that drives your character as they make choices throughout your plot.

Try to recognise which of the seven structures fits your narrative best and familiarise yourself with examples as a baseline for development. There is no need to slavishly follow any of these outlines, but there is also no harm in studying these time-tested forms.

1. Overcoming the Monster
battling the beast

The 5000-year-old *Epic of Gilgamesh* and the first Bond film, *Dr No*, 1962, may be millennia apart, but they are both about **Overcoming the Monster**. Booker describes this timeless plot as unfolding in five stages:

1. **Anticipation Stage and Call**: We become aware of the monster, usually from a great distance. Sometimes we glimpse its destructive power. The hero accepts the call to defeat it.
2. **Dream Stage**: The hero prepares/trains for the battle to come. The distance between him and the monster decreases. All goes well.
3. **Frustration Stage**: We finally come face to face with the monster. The hero seems powerless against such a strong opponent.
4. **Nightmare Stage**: The final ordeal begins, a climactic battle against all the odds. But, just when all seems lost, there is a **Reversal**.
5. **Thrilling Escape from Death / Death of the Monster**.

The monster doesn't have to be an obvious one. Indeed, it may take

> *…human form (e.g., a giant or a witch); the form of an animal (a wolf, a dragon, a shark); or a combination of both (the Minotaur, the Sphinx). It is always deadly, threatening destruction to those who cross its path … the monster often also has in its clutches some great prize, a priceless treasure or a beautiful 'Princess'…* Ibid

Examples include: *Perseus and Medusa*, *Theseus and the Minotaur*, *David and Goliath*, *Beowulf*, *The Thirty Nine Steps*, *Dracula* (vampire), *The Guns of Navarone* (Nazis), *Jurassic Park* (dinosaurs), *King Kong* (gorilla), *The Towering Inferno* (fire), *War of the Worlds* (aliens), *The Day of the Triffids* (plants), *Terminator* (robot), *Jaws* (shark), *Star Wars* (dad), *Avatar* (corporation).

2. RAGS TO RICHES
nothing to lose

Everyone loves a success story, a tale of someone starting from nowhere and beating the odds to win the prize. Booker explains:

> We see an ordinary, insignificant person, dismissed by everyone as of little account, who suddenly steps to the centre of the stage, revealed to be someone quite exceptional.

Whether we follow an individual from childhood into adulthood, or focus on a special time in their life, this plot evolves through five key stages:

1. **INITIAL WRETCHEDNESS AT HOME**: We find the young hero or heroine in their lowly, unhappy state, often overshadowed by malevolent 'dark' figures, who scorn or maltreat them. Then comes **THE CALL** …

2. **OUT INTO THE WORLD, INITIAL SUCCESS**: Pushed out into the world, there are some new ordeals, but also the first taste of success and often some prevision of an eventual glorious destiny.

3. **THE CENTRAL CRISIS**: Everything suddenly goes wrong. The shadows cast by the dark figures return and must be overcome.

4. **INDEPENDENCE & THE FINAL ORDEAL**: The protagonist emerges from the crisis in a new light. A final test, often a battle against the dark figure who stands between them and their goal, forms the climax.

5. **FINAL UNION, COMPLETION & FULFILMENT**: Reward is usually a state of complete union with the prince(ss) or realisation of the truth.

Popular examples of the form include: *The Arthurian Tale of Sir Gareth, Yusuf and Zulaika, The Sword in the Stone, Aladdin, Oliver Twist, Jane Eyre, Rebecca, Pygmalion, The Ugly Ducking, Cinderella, Dick Whittington, David Copperfield, The Gold Rush, Trading Places, Slumdog Millionaire.*

3. Voyage & Return
down the rabbit hole and back again

Voyage and return stories involve characters falling into unfamiliar environments, and encountering otherworldly adventures, before being catapulted back again, changed and improved. Their key stages are:

1. **ANTICIPATION AND 'FALL' INTO THE OTHER WORLD**: The central figure(s) are opened to a new experience. By a **FLIGHT OF FANCY**, or because of **REJECTION** or a need to **ESCAPE**, they are transported out of their familiar existence into a strange new world.
2. **INITIAL FASCINATION OR DREAM**: Exploration of this puzzling and unfamiliar world is exhilarating at first, but makes them uneasy.
3. **FRUSTRATION STAGE**: The adventure becomes frustrating and oppressive. A shadow intrudes and becomes increasingly powerful.
4. **NIGHTMARE STAGE**: The shadow dominates and threatens survival.
5. **THRILLING ESCAPE AND RETURN**: As the threat becomes critical, the heroes escape back home, changed.

Flights of fancy include *Peter Pan*, *Alice in Wonderland*, *The Wizard of Oz*, *Peter Rabbit*, *The Lion, the Witch and the Wardrobe*, *Gulliver's Travels* and *The Time Machine*. Rejections and escapes include *Gone with the Wind*, *Robinson Crusoe*, *The Lord of the Flies* and *Brideshead Revisited* (in these stories the protagonists often need to learn some lesson).

4. The Quest
it's all about the journey

When characters undergo challenging journeys (physical or mental) in search for an ultimate reward, they are probably on a quest. The reward may be a 'promised land' (*Watership Down*, *The Pilgrim's Progress*, *Exodus*), an object (the golden fleece in *Jason and the Argonauts*), knowledge (*The Hitchhiker's Guide to the Galaxy*) or a mythical prize (unholy power in William Beckford's *Vathek*). Booker identifies five key stages in a quest:

1. **THE CALL**: Home has become dull or intolerable. The hero needs to go on a long, difficult journey. He or she is given supernatural or visionary direction towards a distant, life-renewing goal.

2. **THE JOURNEY BEGINS**: The hero, with companions, sets out across hostile terrain, encountering life-threatening ORDEALS or TRIALS.

3. **ARRIVAL AND FRUSTRATION**: The company arrive, seemingly within sight of the goal, but new obstacles loom up which need to be overcome before the goal can be secured.

4. **THE FINAL ORDEALS**: There are a series of tests, often three. Only the hero can complete the final one, proving them worthy of the prize. There may be a dangerous escape.

5. **THE GOAL**: The goal is achieved. Something is retrieved, destroyed or acquired—a kingdom, prince(ss) or life-transforming treasure. Maybe something else entirely.

In many quests, stage 2, the journey, takes up the lion's share of the story. For example, TRIALS can take many forms. There may be DIFFICULT TERRAIN, such as the Mines of Moria in Tolkien's *The Hobbit*, or MONSTERS, such as the elephant in *King Solomon's Mines*. **TEMPTATIONS** may arise, e.g. in *The Odyssey*, Odysseus must escape the hypnotic Sirens, captivating Calypso, and the indulgent illusions of the Lotus Eaters, all of which test the hero's internal strength. Protagonists often have to tread a narrow path between **DEADLY OPPOSITES** with peril on both sides, or voyage to **THE UNDERWORLD** to receive assistance from spirits.

COMPANIONS also add depth to a story. Where would Don Quixote be without Sancho Panza, Hamlet without Horatio, or Frodo Baggins without faithful Sam? A hero, Aristotle tells us, can be hubristic and impulsive, so the chief companion should embody the characteristics they lack, each complementing the other to form a whole

HELPERS can appear along the way, as old wise men or beautiful women, giving the travellers an essential boost, e.g. Galadriel in *Lord of the Rings*, or Virgil and Beatrice in Dante's *Divine Comedy*.

It is often good to be wary of 'promised lands', like Caanan flowing with milk and honey, or the rabbits' all too perfect Watership Down, for it is not until their dangerous ordeal is over that the protagonists (older and wiser) can claim their spiritual and material reward. Thus, it seems, as in life, the journey is often the most important aspect of the story.

Examples of quests in cinema include: *The Adventures of Robin Hood*, the *Indiana Jones* movies, *The Princess Bride*, *Finding Nemo*, *O Brother, Where Art Thou?*, *Princess Mononoke*, *The Fisher King*, *Pirates of the Caribbean: Curse of the Black Pearl*.

5. TRAGEDY
if only

We all experience bad days, but a good tragedy reminds us that things could be *so* much worse. Booker describes the key stages in tragedy as:

1. **ANTICIPATION**: The hero or heroine is unfulfilled. Something is missing. They fixate on some object of desire or course of action to make them complete (e.g. power, fame or a lover).

2. **DREAM**: The hero becomes committed to their course of action (e.g. Faust signs his pact with the devil, Humbert causes the death of Lolita's mother which enables him to start his affair). For a while the desire is gratified, and things go improbably well.

3. **FRUSTRATION**: Small things begin to go wrong. Restless and frustrated, the hero over-reacts, committing further 'dark acts' which make salvation less and less likely. A 'shadow figure' may appear at this point, seeming in some obscure way to threaten him.

4. **NIGHTMARE**: Things now slip out of control. The plan unravels. Fear and despair dominate as fate and the forces of opposition close in.

5. **DESTRUCTION OR DEATH WISH**: Either by external forces or some final act of violence (i.e. murder or suicide), the hero is destroyed. Few people mourn, the darkness dissipates and people rejoice.

Tragedies often begin in much the same way as **RAGS TO RICHES** or **QUEST** stories, but **THE CALL** is more of a **TEMPTATION**, and so the plot follows a markedly different trajectory:

> *Each of these stories shows a hero being tempted or impelled into a course of action which is in some way dark or forbidden.* The Seven Basic Plots, Christopher Booker, 2004

The nature of the **TRAGIC HERO** is also far more complex. Booker explores the idea of **THE HERO AS MONSTER**—expanding on Aristotle's idea of **HAMARTIA** (*see page 4*). From *Icarus* to *Dorian Grey*, this character flaw usually lies in a personal **HUBRIS** (Aristotle's term again), or vanity, with pride inevitably coming before the fall (literal in Icarus' case).

Also, as a tragic hero succumbs to the temptation, they can develop a 'divided self' and a moral division, embodied in Fin de Siècle texts like *Dr Jekyll and Mr Hyde* and *The Picture of Dorian Grey*.

To make something truly tragic, says Booker, bad events must also happen to innocent bystanders:

> In tragedies centred on a hero, we may single out four types of victim who are particularly likely to suffer as a result of the hero's reckless course. Two of these are male, two female - and we may describe them as: the Good Old Man, the Rival or 'Shadow', the Innocent Young Girl, the Temptress. *Ibid*

In Shakespeare we find them all: Polonius from *Hamlet* is our **GOOD OLD MAN**; Duncan in *Macbeth* is **THE RIVAL**; Desdemona in *Othello* is **THE INNOCENT GIRL**; and Cleopatra is **THE TEMPTRESS** in *Antony and Cleopatra*.

Other tragedies include: *Antigone*; *Abelard & Heloise*; *Romeo & Juliet*; *Julius Caesar*; *King Lear*; *Phaedra*; *Faust*; *Don Giovanni*; *Carmen*; *Tristan & Isolde*; *Anna Karenina*; *Tess of the D'Urbervilles*, *Hedda Gabler*; *Wuthering Heights*; *Lolita*; *Frankenstein*, *The Great Gatsby*; *Death of a Salesman*; *Bonnie and Clyde*, *Jules & Jim* and *Titanic*.

6. COMEDY
upside down for a spell

Traditionally, a comedy was a play with a happy ending (often marriage), with some lost or 'incomplete' characters undergoing various confusions and revelries before returning to normal. Shakespeare's *Twelfth Night* is a prime example. In Elizabethan England, Twelfth Night (5th January) was a night of inversion, where a *Lord of Misrule* (usually a peasant) presided over a drunken evening of free speech and release from social hierarchies. Much like the Roman Saturnalia, all rules were suspended for a night.

Modern comedy serves a similar function today, allowing people to laugh at things they would normally find gross (*bathroom comedy*), interesting (*comedy of ideas*), annoying (*comedy of manners*), unsettling (*black comedy*), absurd (*farce*), stupid (*slapstick*), serious (*parody*), humdrum (*observational comedy*) or typical (*situational comedy*).

Booker outlines three stages in classical comedies:

1. **THE SHADOW OF CONFUSION**: People live in a little world in uncertainty and frustration, shut off from one another in various ways.

2. **THE CONFUSION GROWS**: until everyone is in a total tangle.

3. **THE CONFUSION IS LIFTED**: Light reveals all, banishes the shadows and miraculously transforms the situation. There is joyful union.

Examples of the genre (classical and modern) include *Tom Jones*, *The Life and Opinions of Tristram Shandy*, *Pride and Prejudice*, *Three Men in a Boat*, *Carry On Jeeves*, *The Importance of Being Earnest*, *Scoop*, *Fear and Loathing in Las Vegas*, *Duck Soup*, *Some Like it Hot*, *Fawlty Towers*, *Monty Python and the Holy Grail*, *Animal House*, *Airplane*, *Four Weddings and a Funeral* and *Hot Fuzz*.

7. REBIRTH
emerging from the darkness

Everyone gets in a hole sometimes. With a little bit of help, some of us get out again. As always, Booker provides a basic sequence:

1. **THE SPELL OF DARKNESS**: For some reason, maybe initially useful to them, our lead character falls under the shadow of a dark power.
2. **THE STATUS QUO**: For a while, all proceeds reasonably well. The dark power has helped them and its threat appears to have receded.
3. **THE THREAT RETURNS**: The hero or heroine may now see the error of their ways, but the dark power tightens its agonising grip on them.
4. **NO END IN SIGHT**: This goes on for ages. They are imprisoned in a state of living death. The dark power seems to own them.
5. **REDEMPTION**: If the imprisoned figure is female she is miraculously freed by a hero, if male by a young woman or a child.

The protagonist thus enters a kind of chrysalis state from which they emerge stronger and wiser. The suspended animation is necessary as a test of character and to allow full appreciation of the final reward.

Examples include: *Sleeping Beauty*, *Snow White*, *The Frog Prince*, *Beauty and the Beast*, *The Snow Queen*, *A Christmas Carol*, *Crime and Punishment*, *Silas Marner*, *The Secret Garden*, *Fidelio* and *Peer Gynt*.

CHRONOLOGY
making the best use of time

One of the privileges afforded to the writer is manipulation of time to suit their agendas. Film theorist Christian Metz [1931–1993] writes:

> There is the time of the thing told and the time of the narrative (the time of the SIGNIFIED and the time of the SIGNIFIER). This duality [renders] possible all the temporal distortions that are commonplace in narratives (three years of the hero's life summed up in two sentences of a novel or in a few shots of a frequentative montage in film). The Imaginary Signifier (1977)

Theoretician Gunther Muller likewise refers to the opposition between **STORY TIME** and **NARRATIVE TIME** (*Erziililtezeit* and *Erziihlzeit*), noting how an author can choose to skim over large swathes of time, highlighting only their fact rather than their content. For example, Homer's *Odyssey* takes place over ten years as the eponymous hero attempts to make his way back to Ithaca after the Trojan war. The story opens with him trapped on the island of the nymph Calypso. Only the last few days are described in detail, with Odysseus otherwise summarising:

> Seven endless years I remained there, always drenching with my tears the immortal clothes Calypso gave me. Homer, The Odyssey, c.700 BC

The distinction between the chronology of a narrative and the chronology of the events behind it was of great interest to the Russian Formalists, an early group of literary theorists. They defined two aspects: **FABULA**, the raw material of the story, the true chronology behind the narrative; and **SYUZHET**, the way the story is organised.

The film *Citizen Kane* is an exemplar: the *fabula* is the chronological story of Kane's life but the *syuzhet* begins with his death and then unfolds in a series of flashbacks (*Analepsis, see next page*), cross-cut with a present day investigation. This temporal manipulation creates irresistible mysteries; the most famous being Kane's dying word "Rosebud!"—uttered right at the beginning of the film but not explained until the final scene. It earned screenwriters Herman J. Mankiewicz and Orson Welles an Academy Award for best screenplay (*see illustrated analysis below*).

When planning a story, many authors find it easiest to first construct a linear narrative of *fabula* that outlines events from beginning to middle to end. Then, once this initial plotline is complete, the narrator(s) can be liberated from the chronology to explore a *syuzhet* full of multiple perspectives and time frames which then create mysteries, tensions and narrative hooks far more compelling than a simple recount of events.

Over the next few pages we will explore the manipulation of time in plot in more detail.

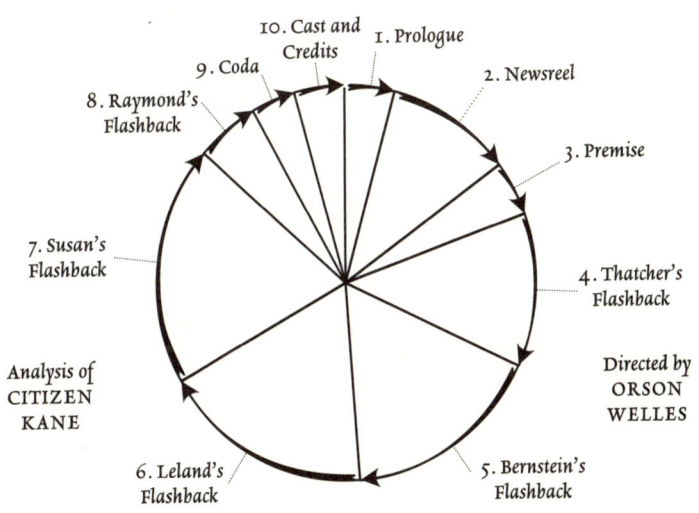

1. Prologue
2. Newsreel
3. Premise
4. Thatcher's Flashback
5. Bernstein's Flashback
6. Leland's Flashback
7. Susan's Flashback
8. Raymond's Flashback
9. Coda
10. Cast and Credits

Analysis of CITIZEN KANE

Directed by ORSON WELLES

Ad Ovo & In Media Res
in the beginning was the middle

In his *Ars Poetica*, written in 13 BC, the Roman writer Horace introduced two key literary terms: *Ab ovo* (from the egg) and *In Media Res* (into the middle of things). So where in the chronology do we start a story?

The 19th century taste for bildungsroman novels (*see page 2*), like Charles Dickens' *David Copperfield*, suggests that audiences can be effectively drawn in to stories which begin *ad ovo*, at the beginning:

> To begin my life with the beginning of my life, I record that I was born (as I have been informed and believe) on a Friday, at twelve o'clock at night. It was remarked that the clock began to strike, and I began to cry, simultaneously.

Dickensian audiences adored his *ad ovo* approach, but many modern readers lack the patience for it; a sentiment expressed brilliantly in the defiant opening to Salinger's *The Catcher in the Rye*:

> If you really want to hear about it, the first thing you'll probably want to know is where I was born, and what my lousy childhood was like, and how my parents were occupied and all before they had me, and all that David Copperfield kind of crap, but I don't feel like going into it, if you want to know the truth. In the first place, that stuff bores me, and in the second place, my parents would have two haemorrhages apiece if I told anything pretty personal about them.

Horace too was unimpressed with such linear plotting. Listing the strengths of Homer's narrative structure in *The Iliad* he comments:

> Nor does he [Homer] begin the Trojan War from the egg, but always he hurries to the action, and snatches the listener into the middle of things....

Another example of *In Media Res*, 'starting in the middle', is Dante's

Divine Comedy which opens Nel mezzo del cammin di nostra vita, 'midway into the journey of our life', with Dante lost in the woods and surrounded by dangers. A further example is J. G. Ballard's opening for his 1975 dystopian novel *High Rise*, which begins:

Later, as he sat on his balcony eating the dog, Dr Robert Laing reflected on the unusual events that had taken place within this huge apartment building during the previous three months.

The technique is particularly prevalent in modern screenwriting. The 2012 James Bond movie *Skyfall* opens with Bond walking tensely down a corridor, pulling his gun, encountering a room of dead and dying men, and then being pursued. Within three minutes of the film opening we are involved in a high-octane car chase through the streets of Istanbul.

In media res chimes with Kurt Vonnegut's advice to writers to 'start as close to the end as possible'. The director Quentin Tarantino does this in many of his films. His 1994 hit, *Pulp Fiction*, begins with the end of the story, a scene in a diner, with the rest of the film then building up to it.

ANALEPSIS & PROLEPSIS
flashbacks and flashforwards

ANALEPSIS, otherwise known as a *flashback*, is where a story goes back to the past, to enrich our understanding of the present by building a character's **BACK STORY** or revealing information crucial to a plot (*see too page 17*). Take, for example, the opening lines of *The Great Gatsby*:

> *In my younger and more vulnerable years my father gave me some advice that I've been turning over in my mind ever since.*
> *"Whenever you feel like criticizing any one," he told me, "just remember that all the people in this world haven't had the advantages that you've had."* F Scott Fitzgerald

Much of the first chapter occurs in flashback, as the narrator Nick Carraway reflects on his own back story, allowing us to get to know him. Here is another example, from near the beginning of *Heart of Darkness*:

> *We looked on, waiting patiently — there was nothing else to do till the end of the flood; but it was only after a long silence, when he said, in a hesitating voice, "I suppose you fellows remember I did once turn fresh-water sailor for a bit," that we knew we were fated, before the ebb began to run, to hear about one of Marlow's inconclusive experiences.* Joseph Conrad

And we do hear about it, as Marlow's story forms the bulk of the novel.

There are many ways of winding back time. While *Citizen Kane* shows one life through the eyes of five different observers (*page 39*), Akira Kurosawa's 1950 epic film *Rashomon* shows four different characters' perspective of the same event, a brutal rape and murder. Each flashback is different, personal to the observer, fallible and questionable. In her bestselling *Harry Potter* novels, author J. K. Rowling uses a *pensieve*, a magical device which enables its user to vividly relive other people's memories, to pop into the past, build back story, and then jump back to the present to unravel the mysteries surrounding the action.

PROLEPSIS, the opposite of analepsis, is a *flash forward* in time. In his poem *Isabella* (reimagined from Boccaccio's *Decameron*) Keats writes:

> So the two brothers and their murder'd man / Rode past fair Florence, to where Arno's stream / Gurgles through straiten'd banks, and still doth fan ...

Two words, "murder'd man", inform us that the gallant hero Lorenzo is riding unassumingly to his death at the hands of the brothers of his betrothed. Dickens uses the device in *A Christmas Carol*, when the Ghost-of-Christmas-Yet-to-Come shows Scrooge his future death, with no-one mourning him, thus precipitating Scrooge's transformation.

Prolepsis is not the same as **PREMONITION**. A flash forward is knowledge of the future given to the audience; a premonition is a vision of the future given to a character. Director Terry Gilliam masterfully combines the two in his 1996 time-travelling masterpiece *Twelve Monkeys*. The film opens with the protagonist, played by Bruce Willis, flashing back to his childhood, where he once saw a man being shot in an airport. It turns out this is also a flash forward, as the man being shot is himself, having travelled back in time to save the world—the scene closing the film.

Foreshadowing
the feeling of what's coming

FORESHADOWING *suggests* what is going to happen, casting a shadow over the narrative (unlike PROLEPSIS, which literally jumps us forward in time). In John Steinbeck's *Of Mice and Men*, the killing of Curley's wife by Lennie is foreshadowed by a litany of such hints. In the opening chapter, Lennie's protector, George, recalls an incident with a woman:

> *"You get in trouble, you do bad things and I got to get you out..." He took on the elaborate manner of little girls when they are mimicking one another. "Jus' wanted to feel that girl's dress — jus' wanted to pet it like it was a mouse — Well, how the hell did she know you jus' wanted to feel her dress? She jerks back and you hold on like it was a mouse. She yells and we got to hide in a irrigation ditch all day..."*

As Lennie's character develops we learn that he is drawn to soft things, fatally unaware of his own strength. First he pets mice:

> *I'd pet 'em, and pretty soon they bit my fingers and I pinched their heads a little and then they was dead - because they was so little.*

Then puppies:

> *Lennie sat in the hay and looked at a little dead puppy that lay in front of him. Lennie looked at it for a long time, and then he put out his huge hand and stroked it, stroked it clear from one end to the other. And Lennie said softly to the puppy, "Why do you got to get killed? You ain't so little as mice. I didn't bounce you hard."*

And finally, tragically but inevitably, Curley's wife. The shadow of death draws over this narrative like storm clouds gathering. Steinbeck uses foreshadowing to create an inevitability to events. As we come to know the characters we can only stand and watch helplessly as events unfold.

There are various ways to allude to the future direction of events:

AUTHORIAL VOICE: The narrator may foreshadow events with a broad brush: "It would be the best day of his life".

DIARY: An event can be diaried or mentioned as approaching, such as an upcoming meeting between two characters, longed for or feared, or a 'big day', such as a performance or battle.

PROPS AND ABILITIES: The presence of a gun tends to foreshadow its use (*see Chekov's Gun, page 50*). The same goes for a flaw, gift or skill.

SPARK: A character may insult or wound another and walk away, creating a shadow of unresolved business. Or, two people can briefly meet and create a more friendly tension.

CONCERN: Parental concern, or lack of concern where there should be concern, can foreshadow an accident.

EXPRESSION: A sad, worried or fearful character can foreshadow our discovery of the disturbance.

PREDICTION: Of the future, via another character voicing their opinion, or by reading a horoscope.

ENVIRONMENT: Bogs, fog and storm clouds are popular devices.

SYMBOLISM: Small symbolic details of the world around, occasionally revisited, can build connections and foreshadow events, e.g. Hemingway's

The leaves fell early that year. A Farewell to Arms

ANAPHORIC & CATAPHORIC
links back and forward

ANAPHORIC and CATAPHORIC references are words, phrases, symbols or motifs which create links, backwards and forwards respectively, to other parts of a story. The terms derive from grammar, e.g. in the sentence *She says she's been training, but I don't believe it!* the pronoun 'it' is an anaphoric reference to the verb 'training', and in the equivalent *She says she has, but I don't believe she's been training!* the verb 'has' is a cataphoric reference to 'training'.

A good example of an anaphoric reference is Harry Potter's scar. Every time his 'scar' is mentioned we are reminded of his mother's sacrifice, his unlikely survival and his unresolved connection with Voldemort:

> *Harry lay flat on his back, breathing hard as though he had been running. He had awoken from a vivid dream with his hands pressed over his face. The old scar on his forehead, which was shaped like a bolt of lightning, was burning beneath his fingers as though someone had just pressed a white-hot wire to his skin.*
>
> J. K. Rowling, *Harry Potter and the Goblet of Fire*.

Anaphoric references can make great plot devices. Apart from signalling and directing attention, they also remind an audience how far the story has come since they last encountered the symbol or phrase. Later appearances in the text can further illuminate the initial mention.

A simple example of a cataphoric reference occurs in the opening line of Carson McCullers' *The Member of the Wedding*:

> *It happened that green and crazy summer when Frankie was twelve years old.*

This is cataphora in that the 'it' pronoun is not explained until later in the text. Instead it is employed deliberately at the start to draw in the reader—what is the 'it' that our speaker is referring to? The anonymity of the pronoun gives the impression that the event is painful in the memory of the narrator, and we move forward searching for clues.

Hilary Mantel uses cataphora in the opening to her novel *Beyond Black*, many of the allusions making little initial sense:

> Travelling: the dank oily days after Christmas. The motorway, its wastes looping London: the margin's scrub grass flaring orange in the lights, and the leaves of the poisoned shrubs striped yellow-green like a cantaloupe melon. Four o'clock: light sinking over the orbital road. Teatime in Enfield, night falling on Potter's Bar.
>
> There are nights when you don't want to do it, but you have to do it anyway. Nights when you look down from the stage and see closed stupid faces. Messages from the dead arrive at random. You don't want them and you can't send them back. The dead won't be coaxed and they won't be coerced. But the public has paid its money and it wants results.

In the opening paragraphs, we skip between narrative voices, times and locations, as supernatural voices of the dead are juxtaposed with everyday motorway driving. Then, as the novel progresses, we meet our clairvoyant protagonist, Alison, and come to understand this fractured opening and its cataphoric references to later events.

Cataphoric references can seem insignificant the first time they appear, only to grow in importance every time they are revisited, like dropped crumbs leading towards the gingerbread house at the end.

TWISTS & REVEALS
spoiler alert

A well-executed twist can be the making of a plot. A sudden turn of events or an extraordinary revelation can jerk a narrative into a completely new direction, or throw everything into an entirely new light—past, present and future. Most twists centre around a character or relationship, with protagonists often being just as shocked as we are about the twist, allowing us to process our emotional reactions through theirs.

A good example occurs in Charlotte Brontë's *Jane Eyre*, where Jane's discovery about the true cause of the noises in the attic leads her to leave the man she loves to process what he has done. Or, in *Star Wars V: The Empire Strike Back*, when the evil Darth Vader reveals to the hero Luke Skywalker "I am your father", a twist which significantly alters our perspective of previous events. Sometimes cataphoric clues foreshadow a twist, as with the final gender-flipping twist in Iain Banks's novel *The Wasp Factory*.

Sometimes, it is our narrator who is tricked by a sudden twist midway through the novel; Sarah Waters uses this device in *The Fingersmith*. Other times it is the narrator who is not what they seem; Gillian Flynn uses an unreliable narrator in her bestselling *Gone Girl*, as does Lionel Shriver in *We Need to Talk About Kevin* and Ian McEwan in *Atonement*.

Comic writer Alec Worley identifies five kinds of twist:

1. **TWIST OF IDENTITY:** Someone (or something) is revealed to be *someone* else, like a father or mother (*Oedipus Rex*), or a son or daughter (*Old Boy*), or *something* else, like a ghost (*Sixth Sense*), a clone (*Oblivion*), a vampire (*From Dusk til Dawn*), an alien, a robot (*Alien*), a virtual reality simulation (*The Thirteenth Floor*), or purely imaginary (*Fight Club*).

2. **TWIST OF MOTIVE:** Someone's intentions are suddenly revealed to be

quite different. In *Harry Potter and the Deathly Hallows*, J. K. Rowling reveals that the seemingly unpleasant Snape has been keeping Harry safe all along, a gut-wrenching twist. In Daphne du Maurier's *Rebecca*, the sobering truth about the eponymous Rebecca and the narrator's husband is revealed as the twist at the end of the novel.

3. **TWIST OF PERCEPTION**: The scales fall from our eyes. Everything is revealed to be as it truly is. At the start of *The Truman Show*, we believe in Truman's world; then learn it's a hoax; then Truman learns the same.

4. **TWIST OF FORTUNE**: A character's fortune turns out to be the opposite of what was expected. Most often a pivotal moment of bad luck.

5. **TWIST OF FULFILMENT**: An apparent gain by one character is suddenly matched or snatched at the last moment by an opposing character.

Devices which can help deliver a successful twist include: **RED HERRINGS**, which can distract the reader with other potential twists or suspicions; **MISGUIDED FOCUS**, where a large part of a story highlights what is in reality a less significant part of the narrative, and **DEAD ENDS**, anticipated twists which come to nothing and make the audience wary of overthinking.

Rachel Scheller of *Writer's Digest* advises:

Readers want their emotional investment to pay off. The twist should never occur in a way that makes them feel tricked, deceived, or insulted. Great twists always deepen, never cheapen, readers' investment in the story.

THE CLIFFHANGER
what happens next?

The *One Thousand and One Nights* uses a simple device to stitch together its ancient collection of tales. A disillusioned Sultan, Shahryar, marries a different virgin every night only to have her executed the next morning. Finally, there is no-one left but Scheherazade. To survive, on their marriage night she starts telling Shahryar a story but does not finish it:

> *Shahryar, who had been listening to Scheherazade with pleasure, said to himself, "I will wait until to-morrow; I can always have her killed when I have heard the end of her story." … As the second night came, Shahrya said to Scheherazade "Finish the story of the genius and the merchant. I am curious to hear the end." So Scheherazade went on with the story. This happened every morning — the Sultana told a story, and the Sultan let her live to finish it the following night.*

Pausing a story unresolved, with a leading character in danger and the reader or viewer anxious to find out what happens next, is known as a CLIFFHANGER. The term comes from Thomas Hardy's serialised novel *A Pair of Blue Eyes*, when the protagonist, Henry Knight, rescues damsel-in-distress Elfride from a cliff face, only to leave himself hanging there:

> 'Elfride, how long will it take you to run to Endelstow and back?'
> 'Three-quarters of an hour.'
> 'That won't do; my hands will not hold out ten

> *minutes. And is there nobody nearer?'*
> *'No; unless a chance passer may happen to be.'*
> *'He would have nothing with him that could save me. Is there a pole or stick of any kind on the common?'*
> *She gazed around. The common was bare of everything but heather and grass.*
> *A minute — perhaps more time — was passed in mute thought by both. On a sudden the blank and helpless agony left her face. She vanished over the bank from his sight. Knight felt himself in the presence of a personalized loneliness.*

Our hero seems to be in dire straits, with little hope of rescue. Hardy cannily makes it imperative that readers purchase the next instalment.

An inversion of the device can also be effective. Towards the end of the first season of the *Games of Thrones* series, the hero Ned Stark finds himself facing public beheading with his two young daughters watching. Expecting a cliffhanger, we wait for his salvation, or for the credit music to roll. However, in defiance of expectation, writers Benioff and Weiss simply see the scene through. Ned loses his head, and the music plays.

Here are ten types of common cliffhanger:

1. **DANGER**: *Man on ledge; Avalanche; Guns pointed; Gang / Police arrive.*
2. **ACCIDENT**: *Car or bike crash; Said the wrong thing; Alarm goes off.*
3. **SURPRISE**: *Twist; Double cross; Revelation; UFO lands; New information.*
4. **RUNNING OUT**: *Of Time, Air, Water, Food, Fuel, Ammo, Blood, Options.*
5. **THREAT / CARROT**: *Monster still alive; Bomb / Nearly kissed, Nearly arrived.*
6. **LOST / FOUND**: *Lost Keys, Baby, Phone / Found Letter, Knife, Bra, Treasure.*
7. **A FOREBODING**: *Looming battle; Pensive plotting; Knock on door; Vow.*
8. **HOPE / HOPELESS**: *Promised, Saved, Solved / Trapped, Captured, Rejected.*
9. **A QUESTION**: *Where (were you last night)? Why? Who? When? But how?*
10. **UNCERTAINTY**: *Did they die? What's in the box? A Dilemma; A False lull.*

PLOTTED OBJECTS
Chekhov's Gun and Macguffins

Some plots make great use of a particular object; sometimes this object is important in itself, but sometimes it isn't at all. The Russian playwright Anton Chekhov [1860–1904] advised writers:

> *Remove everything that has no relevance to the story. If you say in the first act that there is a rifle hanging on the wall, in the second or third act it absolutely must go off. If it's not going to be fired, it shouldn't be hanging there.*

The principle of **CHEKHOV'S GUN** implies that a writer won't make false promises to a reader by introducing elements that are unexplained. If you draw attention to something, you will eventually reveal why you did. Chekhov uses the device in his play *The Seagull*, when just before the midpoint the central character Konsantin enters the stage carrying a gun and a seagull he has shot. At the end of the play, the bird and the weapon make a tragic reappearance, creating a cohesive and cyclical narrative.

Charles Dickens [1812–1870] obeys the rule in *Great Expectations*, introducing the ragged escaped convict Magwitch in the first chapter, who then disappears from the story, only to reappear later as Pip's mysterious benefactor. Another example occurs in Luc Besson's 1997 blockbuster *The Fifth Element*, when, near the beginning, the protagonist Corbin Dallas lights a cigarette, revealing that his matchbox only has one match left. At the end of the film the fate of the world hangs on this one match.

Writer William Faulkner [1897-1962] famously advised writers to "Murder your darlings", i.e. despite being particularly pleased with some section of writing, if it is not aiding the narrative then it needs to be cut, a lesson still taught to scriptwriters and journalists today.

The vapid sibling to Chekhov's Gun object is a **MACGUFFIN**, a motivating object or idea whose identity is actually insignificant. The director Alfred Hitchcock defined it as "The thing that the spies are after but the audience don't care." The search for the Macguffin drives the plot, rather than character development. A good way of telling whether something is a Macguffin or not is to see if it is interchangeable—does it matter if the object is a Fabergé egg, a painting by Picasso, or a memory stick with some amazing new science on it? If the answer is no, then what the object is has no bearing on the actual plot, and it is a Macguffin.

In the classic Bond film, *The Man with the Golden Gun*, the villain Scaramanga, played by Christopher Lee, steals a mysterious device called a solex agitator, which Bond spends the majority of the film attempting to steal back from him. Apart from it being powerful and dangerous in the wrong hands, we really have no idea what it is or how it works, and it doesn't matter—it provides the excuse for the quest.

In *Harry Potter and the Philosopher's Stone*, the eponymous stone is insignificant to the plot, it could be anything with magical powers of resurrection.

In Dashiell Hammett's 1930 novel, *The Maltese Falcon*, the Macguffin, *A glorious golden falcon encrusted from head to foot with the finest jewels*, allows us to concentrate more on the complexities of the characters than the thing that they are chasing, in a plot where everyone is potentially guilty and nothing is at stake.

"The problem is there's no engine. Just a mysterious plot device."

LOCK-INS & BREAKOUTS
deus ex machina

There may be reasons why a character becomes locked into a narrative, e.g. curiosity, honour or some critical point of no return, similar to Aristotle's peripeteia (*see page xx*). But there are other times when there needs to be much more motivation, which is why some writers opt for a **LOCK-IN**.

The writer Agatha Christie [1890–1976] was very fond of this device. In *And Then There Were None* (the world's best-selling mystery novel, and sixth best-selling title of all time), ten people are stuck in a house on a small island off the Devon coast, so when the killing starts there is nowhere to go. In another of her mysteries, *Murder on the Orient Express*, the crime occurs on the train, which limits both the escape options for the perpetrator(s) and the deductive options for Chief Inspector Hercule Poirot.

Lock-ins are very popular amongst film-makers. In Ridley Scott's 1979 science-fiction film *Alien*, the team of astronauts are effectively trapped on their spaceship and have no escape from the monster. *The Shawshank Redemption*, 1995, mostly takes place in a prison. In J. J. Abram's 2011 hit *Super 8*, the characters are bound by a secret. Quentin Tarantino uses the device in his 2015 film *The Hateful Eight*, in which eight strangers seek refuge from a blizzard in a small inn, the majority of the action then taking place in one room. Many horror movies follow the same pattern, requiring an isolated cabin in the woods, a broken-down car or cut phone lines—otherwise the characters can just run away or call the police for help.

While some devices lock characters in, other devices break them out. In **DEUS EX MACHINA** ('God out of the Machine'), a solution to a seemingly unsolvable problem appears suddenly as if by magic. The Greek writer

Euripides [480–406 BC] uses this device. In his play *Orestes*, when all seems lost and the palace is ablaze, the god Apollo suddenly appears, winched down from above, and decreeing what must be done:

> Go your ways, and honour Peace, most fair of goddesses; I, meantime, will escort Helen to the mansions of Zeus, soon as I reach the star-lit firmament.

In *Lord of the Flies*, William Golding has a naval officer in a similar role, appearing in front of the degenerate children like a god. At the end of *The War of the Worlds*, H. G. Wells kills off his alien invasion with a simple bacterial infection. In *The Hobbit* and *The Lord of the Rings*, J. R. R. Tolkien repeatedly uses eagles to rescue his protagonists when all seems lost.

The evil twin of Deus ex Machina is **DIABOLUS EX MACHINA** ('Devil from the Machine'), where events take a downward turn as a malevolent force intervenes. Things suddenly get worse for the protagonist, or the antagonist, or both. A good example occurs in Matthew Lewis's 1796 Gothic tale *The Monk*, where the antagonist's crimes are so great that the devil himself appears to resolve the situation.

While most diabolous events occur at the end of narratives, they can be used earlier on too. Roald Dahl used them with playful flippancy throughout his books, cutting through plot hurdles in an almost self-satirising way:

> *One day, a terrible thing happened. A giant rhinoceros came out of nowhere and gobbled up his poor mother and father.*
>
> James and the Giant Peach, 1996

PLOTTING A PLOT
plan in detail, or go with the flow

Some writers plan meticulously with clever foreshadowing and a tight focus to produce work that is concise and cohesive. Others rely on their characters to shape their narratives as they go along, producing work that can be more original, experimental, immediate and realistic.

> *I always have a basic plot outline, but I like to leave some things to be decided while I write.* J. K. Rowling

> *Outlines are the last resource of bad fiction writers who wish to God they were writing masters' theses.* Stephen King

Like many authors, J. K. Rowling uses a table to plan her story (*upper, opposite*), with dates down the left side, and columns for plot, subplots, character groups and characters, e.g. there is a column for the **PROPHECY** subplot that appears in some chapters, and another for the **CHO/GINNY** romance subplot which weaves through the book. Although more detailed, Joseph Heller's outline for *Catch 22* uses a similar structure (*lower, opposite*). Below we see another format, with a new column for **POINT OF VIEW**.

Possibly the best way to consider plot is to take Ernest Hemingway's typically practical approach to it: *Prose is architecture. It's not interior design.* A plot is indeed like the design for a house. There are basic blueprints which need to be in place before building can begin. Then, essential foundations need to be laid, certain walls need to be built to support others, then stairs and doorways can connect the rooms and floors, etc.

SCENE	POINT OF VIEW	WHERE	WHO IS PRESENT	WHAT HAPPENS	PLOT	SUBPLOTS 1-4	CHARACTER ARCS 1-8
1							

No. Month SCENE   PLOT   SUB PLOTS   GROUPS   PEOPLE

NO	TIME	TITLE	PLOT	PROPHECY	CHO/GINNY	O of P	D.A.	SNAPE/HARRY	HAGRID/GRAWP
13	OCT	Plots & Resistance	Harry, Ron & Hermi go to Hogsmeade, meet Lupin and Tonks - can't talk. Umbridge banning. Will recruiting for D of P. Hagrid fresh injuries.	HALL OF PROPHECY. Harry sees Vol still formulating his plans, those of the Death Eaters able to get in	Cho in Hogsmeade	Tonks - Lupin	Recruiting	Harry ships lessons to recruit for D.A.	Hagrid still getting injuries. Blood claims "It's looking something. That's not his blood?"
14	OCT	Dumbledore's Army	First meeting of Dumbledore's Army.	Scotch, Hagrid on room - his eyes	Cho - Ginny both present	Umbridge now reading their mail	First meeting	Harry still skipping class - Snape not going	
15	NOV	The Dirtiest Tackle	Quidditch versus Slytherin. Harry suspended following attack on Malfoy after Cedric fouled. That night Harry restless, unable to sleep. Worries about Umbridge. Cho, scar. Sees Hagrid attack Mr.	Hagrid attacks Mr. bd	Cho now madly in love	They can see thestrad			
16	NOV	Black Marks	Ron vs skipping Snape lesson, Harry's really in doubtmate. He's angry. Overruns into Xmas. Hermione contacts Rita Snape lesson.	Smiles in dream. Hagrid gets in. Vol has confirmation of Bode's story. Only he and Harry can touch the prophecy	Cho hiss? Ginny concerned about father	Ron - rest of lot, called in to be told of father's injury	Reacting to the attack. Another meeting? Overview	Row about Harry not going	Hagrid still getting injuries
17	DEC	Rita Returns	Hogsmeade / Xmas shopping they meet Rita	Rita information "Pippy skipkey"	Harry now avoiding Cho - Ginny with someone else?		Another lesson		Hagrid hospital wing
18	DEC	St Mungo's Hospital	St Mungo's visit Xmas Eve. See Bode (Placeour anything). See Lockhart. See Mr Weasley. NEVILLE	NOW VOL IS ACTIVELY TRYING TO GET HARRY TO H of P. Very weird. Could	Ginny - Dad	Around			
19	DEC	Xmas		Bode dead. H of P again.	Hermione + Krum. Ginny + boy! Ron	Sirius here. Big reunion			
20	JAN	Extended powers of Elvira Umbridge	Harry misses match v. Hufflepuff. Order of Phoenix now suspected by Umbridge. Why weren't they at the match. Snape lesson?				D.A. Day Meeting	Snape lessons. H mentions H of Prophecy	Hagrid out of hospital now. Going into forest around with spikes etc.
21	FEB	Valentines Day	With Cho. Hogsmeade. Treleaney out. Firenze replaces in midst of time. Rita reports back on Bode etc. Snape lesson?	Harry glimpses horcrucial's (being made) by Vol and Dumb dimpness	Valentine date with Cho - C miserable - they could row		D.A.		
22	FEB	Cousin Grawp	Hagrid now really going for Hagrid. Firenze teaching prophecy and prophecies. HHR go to warn Hagrid about Umbridge. Meet Grawp.			to help Sirius and happily expose greatness	D.A.	Snape going ape at Harry because he can't do it	
23	MAR	Treason	Easter - discovery of Dumbledore's Army. Dumbledore takes the rap vis - Azkaban.		Harry blocking out			Snape grudgingly approves	
24	MAR	Careers Guidance	Careers consultation. Aaron. Dumbledore's Army continues. Ginny has dumped on the wall in temper. Snape lesson.		Harry starting to get how to block his dreams	Firehead	See plot MEETING things hotting up with F-G.		Hagrid clinging onto job. Refusing to abandon Grawp

TIME, a few scenes a month --->

Date EVENT   CHARACTERS   GROUPS   NOTES

TIME, a few scenes a month --->

Upper: Plot grid by J. K. Rowling for Harry Potter and the Order of the Phoenix.
Lower: Joseph Heller's incredibly detailed outline for Catch 22.

53

Expanding a Plot
the snowflake method

Writing advisor Randy Ingermanson's ten step *snowflake method* for expanding a plot is inspired by the *Koch snowflake*—a fractal curve where a simple triangle is built up iteratively until it forms a complex geometrical snowflake (*below*). As with the house-building analogy (*page 54*), you start with a simple outline and then gradually add levels of detail and complexity, interweaving subplots and character development:

1. **Elevator Pitch.** What is your story about? Distil the essence of the narrative down to 15 words or fewer.

2. **Summary Paragraph.** Expand the elevator pitch to a paragraph, describing the beginning, middle and end of the novel, and identifying key reversals and conflicts.

3. **Character Summaries.** Create a summary for *each* of the principal characters in your narrative, with their: name; outline storyline; motivation; goal; conflict; and epiphany. Plus a longer one-paragraph version of their storyline.

4. **Extended Summary.** Develop each sentence of your summary paragraph into a full paragraph in its own right (aim for 1-2 pages).

5. **Characters in Detail.** Memorable characters make a story. Knowing

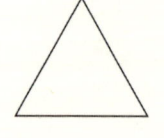

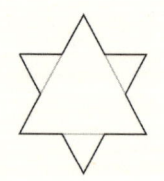

how yours think, move, walk and talk, plus their idiosyncrasies, will help you write them more convincingly. Give a day to each central character to create a 1-2 page detailed profile, with a sketch, family background, habits, etc. These need not appear in the novel, e.g. you might write 'probably a bully at school' but this doesn't mean you need to flash back to their playground days in the course of the narrative.

6. **DETAILED SUMMARY.** Return to Step 4 and turn each paragraph into a whole page, to create a 4-6 page detailed narrative document.

7. **CHARACTER DEVELOPMENT CHARTS.** Return to Step 5 and make a detailed chart or multiple charts, showing how each character evolves and changes over the arc of the narrative. Add *everything* there is to know about each individual.

8. **SPREADSHEET.** Use your detailed summary from Step 6 to create an initial column of key scenes, with a row for each one and multiple columns, headed as you see fit (*see examples on pages 54-55*).

9. **ROUGH** (optional): Ingermanson says: *Take each line of the spreadsheet and expand it to a multi-paragraph description of the scene. Put in any cool lines of dialogue you think of, sketch out the essential conflict of that scene. If there's no conflict, you'll know it here and you should either add conflict or scrub the scene.*

10. **WRITE:** Begin writing. Safely armed with a well developed plot, you should be able to relax and focus on the quality of your expression.

"Write what you know. Write about male-pattern baldness."

Grand Openings
once upon a time

What makes a great first line? Many 19th century novels start with wise words, but these days opening lines tend to be more fast-paced, less wordy. As L.P. Hartley says at the start of his 1953 novel *The Go-Between*: *The past is a foreign country: they do things differently there.* Broadly, there are six types:

1. **Personal (Breaking The Fourth Wall):** *Call me Ishmael.* Moby-Dick (1851)

    My mother died today. Albert Camus, The Stranger (1942)

    If you are interested in stories with happy endings, you would be better off reading some other book. Lemony Snicket, Daniel Handler, A Series of Unfortunate Events (1999)

    In these examples, the narrators address us directly, openly dismissing the conventions of storytelling. We blink, the character invites us in.

2. **Odd:** *124 was spiteful. Full of baby's venom.* Beloved (1987)

    It was a bright cold day in April, and the clocks were striking thirteen. G. Orwell, (1984).

    I write this sitting in the kitchen sink. Dodie Smith, I Capture the Castle (1948)

    These all have a tone of discord, something needs to be resolved.

3. **Reflective:** *Many years later, as he faced the firing squad, Colonel Aureliano Buendía was to remember that distant afternoon when his father took him to discover ice.*
    Gabriel García Márquez, One Hundred Years of Solitude (1967); trans. Gregory Rabassa

    Whether I shall turn out to be the hero of my own life, or whether that station will be held by anybody else, these pages must show. Charles Dickens, David Copperfield (1850)

    Marquez begins with a character reflecting on his past. This compelling opening takes a huge risk—it is the ultimate spoiler. We now know what will happen, but Marquez banks on our compulsion to see how an ice skating child becomes a colonel facing a firing squad.

4. **POETIC:** *Lolita, light of my life, fire of my loins.* <small>Vladimir Nabokov, Lolita (1955)</small>

The sun shone, having no alternative, on the nothing new. <small>Samuel Beckett, Murphy (1938)</small>

On my naming day when I come 12 I gone front spear and kilt a wyld boar he parbly ben the las wyld pig on the Bundel Downs … <small>Russell Hoban, Riddley Walker (1980)</small>

These three examples use phonology, wordplay and dialect to immediately immerse the reader deeply into the world of the story.

5. **DRAMATIC:** *They say when trouble comes close ranks, and so the white people did.* <small>Jean Rhys, Wide Sargasso Sea (1966)</small>

Someone must have slandered Josef K., for one morning, without having done anything truly wrong, he was arrested. <small>Franz Kafka, The Trial (1925); trans. Breon Mitchell</small>

Jean Rhys tells us there is trouble afoot, setting the tone of racial tension which runs throughout the work. Rather than a slow build, Kafka throws us in at the deep end *in media res* (*page 34*).

6. **PROVERBIAL:** *Happy families are all alike; every unhappy family is unhappy in its own way.* <small>Leo Tolstoy, Anna Karenina (1875)</small>

It is a truth universally acknowledged, that a single man in possession of a good fortune, must be in want of a wife. <small>Jane Austen, Pride and Prejudice (1813)</small>

Nineteenth century writers were particularly fond of this method. Often ambiguous, these well-crafted phrases simultaneously set the scene, frame and foreshadow the entire novel by underscoring one of the central themes in the work.

GREAT ENDINGS
happily ever after, maybe

The end of a story is a significant moment. The reader expects to be rewarded with closure, insight or some thought-provoking ambiguity. The examples below demonstrate five broad types of ending:

OPTIMISTIC: *After all, tomorrow is another day.* Gone with the Wind, Margaret Mitchell

The eyes and faces all turned themselves towards me, and guiding myself by them, as by a magical thread, I stepped into the room. The Bell Jar, Sylvia Plath

ACCEPTING: *There was some open space between what he knew and what he tried to believe, but nothing could be done about it, and if you can't fix it, you've got to stand it.*
Brokeback Mountain, Annie Proulx

TAINTED POSITIVE: *She had started to cry softly. Odenigbo took her in his arms.*
Half of a Yellow Sun, C. Adichie

AMBIGUOUS: *"Are there any questions?"* The Handmaid's Tale, Margaret Atwood

"He is coming, and I am here."
The Time Traveller's Wife, Audrey Niffenegger

NEGATIVE: *He loved Big Brother.*
1984, George Orwell

Perhaps the greatest last line ever penned is from *The Great Gatsby*. Its alliterative rhythm manages to encapsulate all five categories.

So we beat on, boats against the current, borne back ceaselessly into the past.
F. Scott Fitzgerald

"It's a novel about loss, and redemption, and fantastic sex."